It was never contemplated to be a college, and that term has never been applied to it. It was intended to provide a place where midshipmen and instructors could be congregated to pursue certain subjects essential to the training of naval officers and to develop those traits of character most desirable to the naval service.

Despite its great growth, despite the changes and expansion in curriculum and activities, despite its enormous influence in the Navy and the nation, it has remained essentially just that to the present day.

Shipmate, October 1945

UNITED STATES

NAVAL ACADEMY

1845

PHOTOGRAPHY BY DAN DRY

HARMONY HOUSE
PUBLISHERS LOUISVILLE

First Edition November, 1987, by Harmony House Publishers
Executive Editors: William Butler and William Strode
Director of Photography: William Strode
ISBN 0-916509-15-X
Library of Congress Catalog Number 86-082737
Printed in U.S.A. by Pinaire Lithographing Corp., Louisville, Kentucky
Copyright © 1987 by Harmony House Publishers
P.O. Box 90, Prospect, Kentucky 40026 (502) 228-2010 / 228-4446
Photographs copyright © 1987 by Dan Dry.
This book or portions thereof may not be reproduced in any form
without permission of Harmony House Publishers.
Photographs may not be reproduced in any form without the
permission of Dan Dry.

Harmony House wishes to thank the U.S. Naval Academy Alumni Association
for its help and enthusiastic support during the production of this book. In
particular, we wish to thank Rear Admiral Ronald F. Marryott, Superintendent,
United States Naval Academy; Captain W.S. Busik, Executive Director, United
States Naval Academy Alumni Association; CDR Stephen Clawson; CDR Kendall
Pease; Dennis Boxx; CDR Edward R. Hebert; James A. Kiser; Midshipman J.M.
Byrne; Assistant Archivist Jane H. Price; and Special Collections Head Alice Creighton.

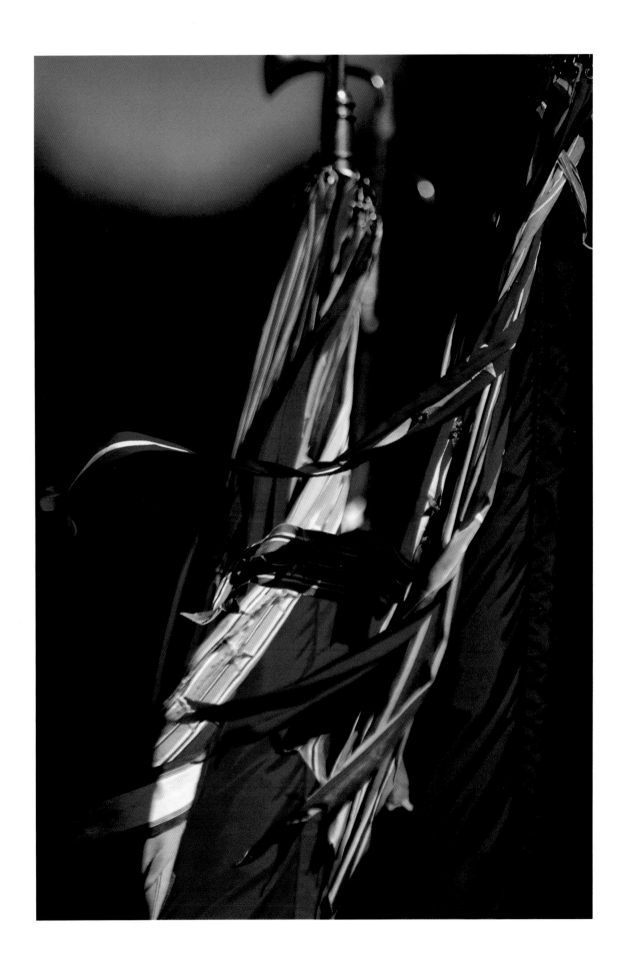

The Chapel

INTRODUCTION

By Robert W. McNitt
Rear Admiral, United States Navy, Retired

The Naval Academy! Seen for the first time by the candidate who had traveled across the country to become a midshipman, it is awesome, intimidating, a bright challenge to be met earnestly and hopefully. Several years later, the beauty of the yard in snow or spring goes unnoticed in the daily demands of class, sports and the expectations of an awaited letter or a weekend away. For an exuberant graduate as caps fly skyward in the relief of success, it is almost ignored in the excitement of the future. And to the homecoming alumnus arriving with family in tow, it suddenly becomes a forgotten friend awakening memories of fun and frolic, the fits and starts of failure and progress that measure growth, and above all of the deep friendships made during shared tribulations and triumphs.

What is there about the Naval Academy that stirs such strong emotions in men and women who have known and loved this place for nearly a hundred and fifty years?

Well, ask one of the more than a million visitors escorted among the monuments in the yard by volunteer tour guides in blue and gold dresses. The word you will hear most often is tradition, and that indeed is the planned heart and soul of the Naval Academy.

Stand in Memorial Hall under the battle flag "Don't Give Up The Ship" flown by Oliver Hazard Perry at the Battle of Lake Erie in 1813 and look over the balcony across the Severn River and Annapolis Harbor. The captured flags and the memorials to heroic warriors of our country's Navy and Marine Corps surround you, and the spectacular view across Chesapeake Bay will almost physically draw you seaward to service and adventure on the oceans and continents of the world.

Attend Sunday service in the magnificent chapel and sense the faith and strength given to generations of midshipmen as the familiar liturgy and music joins the congregation into a family led by inspirational chaplains who themselves are naval officers. Note the moist eyes among those remembering loved ones, friends, and shipmates lost at sea as the Navy hymn swells to its emotional closing. And thrill to the sudden flash of color as the flag bearers fling out the folds of red, white and blue, and of blue and gold, while stepping down the chancel steps.

And of course, visit the crypt of John Paul Jones, the consummate seaman and warrior whose eloquent definition of a proper naval officer carries the same ring of truth today. Observe the bronze bust which caused Lord Jellicoe to observe during a visit to the crypt, "Rather nice face for all the trouble he caused."

Then think for a moment what a unique opportunity is offered here to the youth of our nation. For bright, physically active and adventurous young men and women from every corner of our country, this Academy provides a superb education with an accredited bachelor of science degree, and the professional preparation to enter naval aviation, to serve in ships on the surface and under the sea including training in nuclear propulsion, or world wide service on land, in the air and at sea in the Marine Corps.

And as you leave our gates, think what it means to young men and women far from home to have the warm and welcoming people of charming, colonial Annapolis only a short walk away from their spartan dormitory rooms, the maritime pleasures of Chesapeake Bay, and the attractions of two major cities within an hour's drive.

This is the Naval Academy and Annapolis. A great place to visit, and an even greater place to call home.

BLUE AND GOLD

Now college men from sea to sea
May sing of colors true,
But who has better right than we
To hoist a symbol hue?
For sailor men in battle fair
Since fighting days of old
Have proved a sailor's right to wear
The Navy blue and gold.

So hoist our colors, hoist them high
And vow allegiance true;
So long as sunset gilds the sky
Above the ocean blue,
Unlowered shall those colors be,
Whatever fate they meet,
So glorious in victory
Triumphant in defeat.

Four years together by the Bay
Where Severn joins the tide,
Then by the service called away,
We've scattered far and wide;
But still when two or three shall meet
And old tales be retold,
From low to highest in the fleet
Will pledge the Blue and Gold.

Bancroft Hall

THE PRAYER OF A MIDSHIPMAN

Almighty Father, whose way is the sea, whose paths are in the great waters, whose command is over all, and whose love never faileth: Let me be aware of Your presence and obedient to Your will. Keep me true to my best self, guarding me against dishonesty in purpose and in deed, and helping me so to live that I can stand unashamed and unafraid before my shipmates, my loved ones, and You. Protect those in whose love I live. Give me the will to do my very best and to accept my share of responsibilities with a strong heart and a cheerful mind. Make me considerate of those entrusted to my leadership and faithful to the duties my country has entrusted to me. Let my uniform remind me daily of the traditions of the Service of which I am a part. If I am inclined to doubt, steady my faith; if I am tempted, make me strong to resist; if I should miss the mark, give me the courage to try again. Guide me with the light of truth and keep before me the life of Him by whose example and help I trust to obtain the answer to my prayer, Jesus Christ our Lord, Amen.

Written by Chaplain William N. Thomas, originally presented in 1938

The Chapel

Entering the Academy enclosure — a high wall runs around it except on the two water sides — the visitor is impressed anew with the size and scope of the architectural scheme and the regal beauty and newness of the buildings around him. The immense campus, perfectly kept, and shaded by hundreds of fine old trees, sweeps off toward the Severn, whose waters glisten through the branches. Bancroft Hall and its great wings loom up even larger than from the front.

Littel McClung in *The Evening Capital*, May 1908

Bancroft Hall

On my first day as a plebe I called my father and told him, "I'm leaving here." On the way back from the phone booth I changed my mind and I never looked back.

Admiral Elmo R. Zumwalt

Induction Day

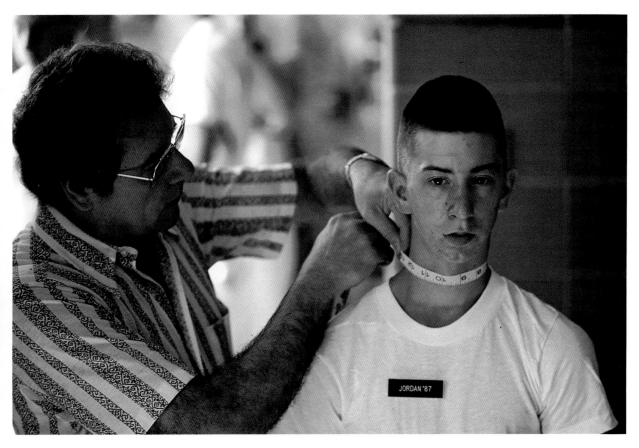

*Leadership is the essence of what we're about — otherwise
we'd send everybody to M.I.T. or Stanford.*

Captain Richard A. Stratton

Talk to your Super about his days in a prisoner-of-war camp and you'll get some feel for the importance he attaches to "learning" in a stressful environment — which is what the Naval Academy is all about – controlled stress. You have developed, whether you know it or not, a special tolerance for pressure as a consequence of the "system", the disciplines that have become an essential part of your character.

Admiral Thomas B. Hayward, Chief of Naval Operations, May, 1980

You are part of a long and deep tradition that you can call on in times of strife and peril. You are steeped in the history and the standards of the world's foremost Navy and Marine Corps team. You inherit a code of perserverance and victory second to none, and it rests on the achievements of men like Farragut, Dewey, Sims, King, Nimitz, Spruance and a host of others. I can testify that there will be times when you personally draw on the Navy's traditions for strength, and that you will find them genuinely sustaining.

Admiral William J. Crowe, Jr. , 1986

To capture this spirit of the sea is a part of this Annapolis tradition. The Naval Academy furnishes the environment and the atmosphere, and the midshipmen must gather the import of it all in a rather osmotic fashion. It cannot be taught, it must be understood and felt ...like religion.

Commander Leland P. Lovette, in *School of the Sea*

Wooden Shoe Regatta

Mahan Hall

When we occasionally revisit the Naval Academy most of us have the heartwarming sense of returning to old friends and familiar scenes. No matter how large the classes grow, no matter what changes occur to Academy buildings and grounds, there is always the pleasant feeling of finding most things as we hoped to find them. The countryside, the bay, the Severn, the city of Annopolis, even the waterfront trees and walls.... all bring back recollections of our early years.

Vice Admiral Wilson Brown

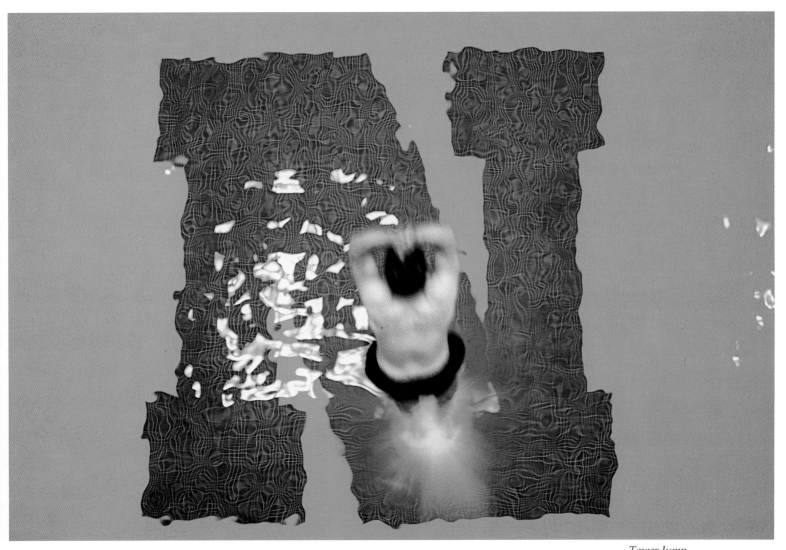

Tower Jump

In four years these boys, gathered together from every state in the Union, from rich families and poor families alike, are expected to become not only educated gentlemen, but international lawyers, keen observers, navigators, artillerists, engineers and also all-around men and specialists. On the whole, the expectation of the people of the United States is justified. On the whole, the United States Naval Academy accomplishes more in four years than any other college in the country.

Franklin D. Roosevelt, from *Life at the United States Naval Academy* by Ralph Earle, 1917

King Hall

None but a Naval officer could fully understand the devotion of another officer to their common service. The close unity of thought and action that binds our profession into a great fraternity has no parallel among civilians.

Rear Admiral Thomas O. Selfridge, Jr.

Memorial Hall

You cannot do better than to follow the example provided for you by the generations of American naval officers whose presence and achievements are everywhere here remembered.

Harold Brown, Secretary of Defense, 1979

The Rotunda

*If there is a Valhalla where the spirits of the heroic dead of the Navy congregate
to hold wassail and to re-live the great exploits that brought them immortality
in the annals of the sea, their gathering place must surely be Memorial Hall.*

Kendall Banning in *Annapolis Today*, 1939

A captain of the Navy ought to be a man of Strong and well connected sense with a tolerable education, a Gentleman as well as a Seaman, both in Theory and in Practice.

John Paul Jones

The Academy is the only place I know which pushes each midshipman to his absolute mental and physical limits. Although I've had my back against the wall, the Academy taught me to bounce back. That's when I started feeling good about the Academy and myself.

Midshipman Kennon Artis

Summer Navy training

Maryland State House / Annapolis

It is obvious to the observing that the alliance of naval and civilian Annapolis constitutes a united combination as they go through the years together, arm in arm — the Naval Academy as the handsome grandson of Old Dame Annapolis.

Shipmate, October 1945

Ring Dance

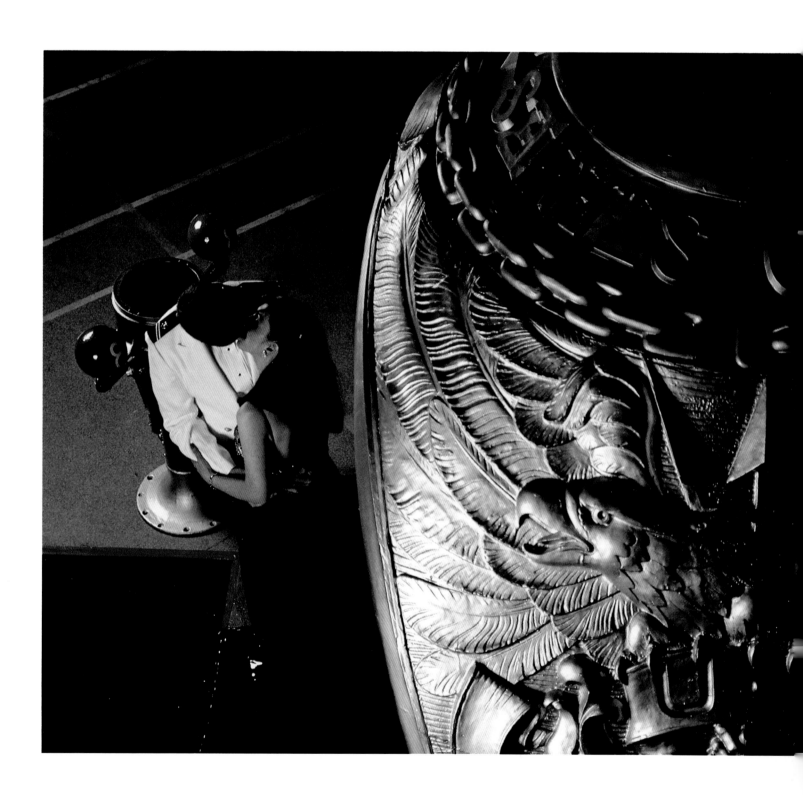

Just before the opening game of the 1902 season, the regular halfback was badly injured and I was put in. I kept the job that season and the next, my last... those two teams were probably the poorest the Academy ever produced. More than 40 years later, General of the Army Eisenhower, whom I had never met before, came up to me in Fleet Admiral King's office in Washington. His first remark was not,"I'm glad to meet you," or,"How are you?" but,"Admiral, they tell me you claim to be the worst fullback that ever went to the Naval Academy." I wasn't sure what this was leading to, so my answer was a bit truculent. "Yes, that's true, what about it?" Eisenhower laughed and stuck out his hand. "I want you to meet the worst halfback that ever went to the Military Academy."

Fleet Admiral William F. Halsey, in *Admiral Halsey's Story*

BEAT ARMY

GO NAVY

ARMY   Merit Gasolines   NAVY

Crew

We develop leadership, moral sense and ethical integrity at the Academy.
We teach people to respond under stress, to develop self-discipline. The education
received here enables our graduates to succeed in or out of the military.

Rear Admiral Leon A. Edney

Herndon Monument

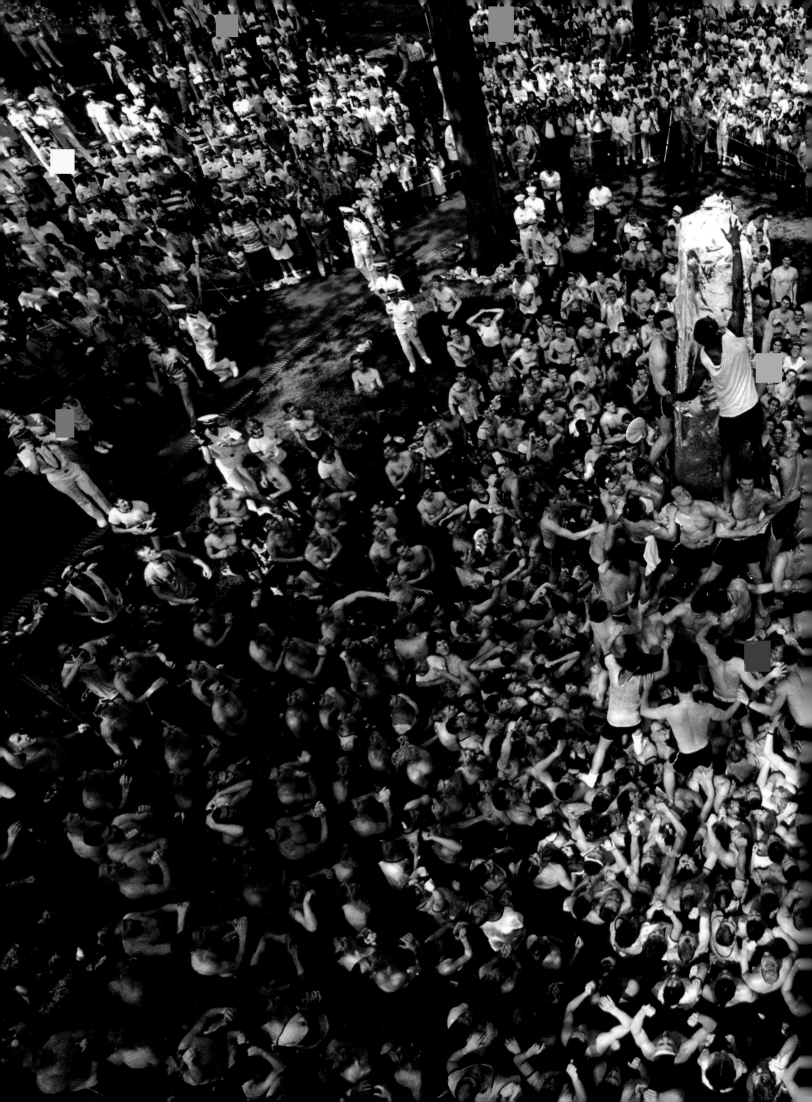

The Tecumseh statue

The average midshipman aquires more information, works and studies more and harder and accomplishes more than the average university student – and the reason for it is that he is almost entirely on his own resources and must dig it out for himself or bilge.

Fleet Admiral Chester W. Nimitz

89

Before you depart this academy that you have known so well, stay a moment, reflect a bit. And when you depart, think occasionally of its ideas and purposes. The right to the pursuit of truth was not given, it was won, earned in conflict, and the fight continues to this day and beyond. Carry away with you some of its timeless courage and unlimited objectivity, which represent the collective input of its founders and students and teachers who have gone before you. It has been, and remains, the obligation of this academy to transmit, from one generation to another, our heritage.

Donald Rumsfeld, Secretary of Defense, 1976

On these hallowed grounds we celebrate a
ritual of passage, a routine as regular as the
coming of spring, and in many ways, as
symbolic. We gather to celebrate the birth
of "new life", the introduction of a new
Class to a life of duty, honor and service.

Vice President George Bush, 1987

REMEMBERING THE NAVAL ACADEMY

A SELECTION OF PHOTOGRAPHS FROM THE ARCHIVES AND SPECIAL COLLECTIONS

During the Civil War the Academy moved its operations from Annapolis to Fort Adams, near Newport, Rhode Island. This building, Atlantic House, was a dormitory for midshipmen from 1861 through 1865. It is shown here circa 1862.

This elaborate landscaping behind Stribling Row provided a park-like setting for walks in 1870.

The men in the picture are identified as members of the class of 1870. They are standing in front of a section of Stribling Row in 1868. Stribling Row included some midshipmen's quarters, the mess hall, the chapel, recitation halls and other academic buildings.

The Academy's main gate in 1890 faced Maryland Avenue. Notice that the guard houses are virtually unchanged from their appearance at this gate today.

An artillery drill in 1892.

In 1887 midshipmen assemble in the street for a formal artillery drill.

The Naval Academy football team posed for this picture in 1894.

A large crowd turned out on this Fall day in 1893 to watch the Academy football team play an unidentified opponent. Three years

Other Naval Academy athletics in 1893 included crew. The Academy made its first appearance at an intercollegiate meet in June of 1907.

earlier, on November 29, 1890, the first Army-Navy football game was played, with the midshipmen winning 20-0.

Speaking at the graduation exercises of 1902 was President Theodore Roosevelt, who also delivered the diplomas to the 59 graduates.

Bancroft Hall was in its early construction stage in this picture from 1902.

This 1904 photograph shows a brand-new Dahlgren Hall to the left, Annapolis residences to the right, and in between, a canal in the making that eventually was used to transport building materials up to the site of the new Chapel.

Midshipmen begin training aboard the submarine *Holland*, 1905.

These steam launches were used for seamanship training at the turn of the century.

This photograph, circa 1905, shows the Chapel under construction, and, in the foreground, the canal that was dug to facilitate the transportation of materials to the building site.

When American naval hero John Paul Jones' body is returned to the United States from an obscure graveyard in France, the Naval

Academy honors the occasion with ceremonies on April 24, 1906. Jones' memorial remains on Academy grounds to this day.

Bancroft Hall, the world's largest dormitory, is shown here in 1918.

The Naval Academy Chapel was completed in 1908, and held its first service on May 24 of that year. This winter view is from 1918.

This 1939 airview shows a rapidly growing Academy; some two years later, 30 more acres are added by pumping silt from the Severn River along an area of the shore secured with steel bulkheads. Eight acres of this reclamation are eventually used as the site of Holland Field.

In celebration of the Academy's 90th Anniversary, a reenactment of the first Army-Navy game is held at Thompson Stadium, 1935.

Midshipmen celebrate V-J Day, August 14, 1945.

Right, a typical midshipman's room of the 1930s.

Below, the Mess Hall in 1950. In this year Vice Admiral Harry W. Hill became Superintendent, and the class of 1950 graduated 691 midshipmen.